TRANSPORT

Written by
Ian Wolseley

Illustrated by
Tony Richards and Graham White

Designed by
Peter Shirtcliffe

Edited by
Alison Cooper

Picture research by
Helen Taylor

CONTENTS

On the move

Stop and think

Imagine a world without transport – no buses, no trains, no cars. How would you visit your friends, go to school or go shopping? Transport is part of our daily lives.

Until about two hundred years ago most people travelled only short distances, usually on foot. Rich and important people travelled further, by coach or on horseback. Technology has helped us move ourselves and the goods we need more easily.

Time travel

A time line shows when events happened. This time line shows you when some of the different forms of transport described in this book were used.

1819
The first ocean-going steamships had paddle wheels. In good winds the sails were used.

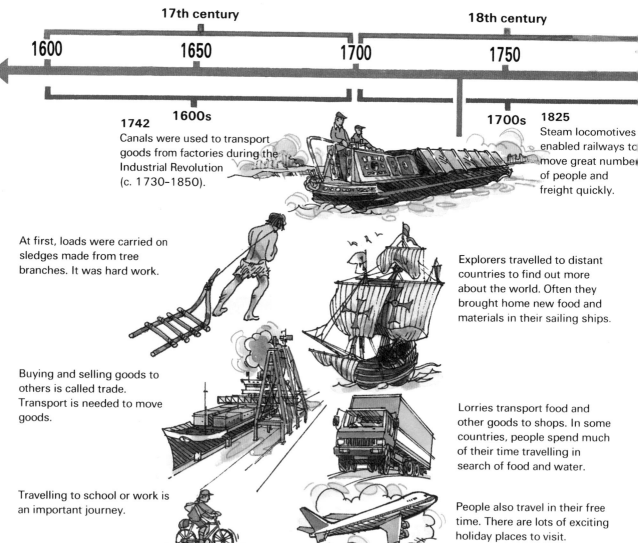

17th century

18th century

1600   1650   1700   1750

1742
1600s
Canals were used to transport goods from factories during the Industrial Revolution (c. 1730–1850).

1700s
1825
Steam locomotives enabled railways to move great number of people and freight quickly.

At first, loads were carried on sledges made from tree branches. It was hard work.

Explorers travelled to distant countries to find out more about the world. Often they brought home new food and materials in their sailing ships.

Buying and selling goods to others is called trade. Transport is needed to move goods.

Lorries transport food and other goods to shops. In some countries, people spend much of their time travelling in search of food and water.

Travelling to school or work is an important journey.

People also travel in their free time. There are lots of exciting holiday places to visit.

Better roads and new types of transport have changed many places. The main picture shows Golders Green, London, in 1904. The inset picture shows the same area in 1991.

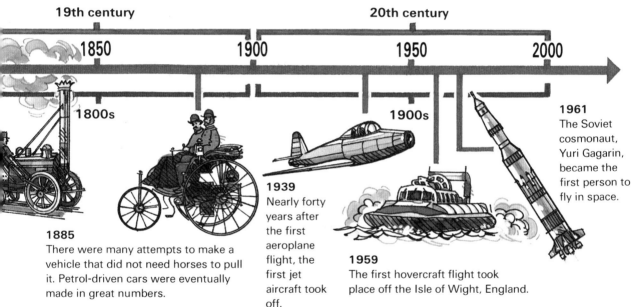

19th century

20th century

1850 1900 1950 2000

1800s

1900s

1961
The Soviet cosmonaut, Yuri Gagarin, became the first person to fly in space.

1939
Nearly forty years after the first aeroplane flight, the first jet aircraft took off.

1959
The first hovercraft flight took place off the Isle of Wight, England.

1885
There were many attempts to make a vehicle that did not need horses to pull it. Petrol-driven cars were eventually made in great numbers.

	Sat 4·00pm	Mon 4·00pm
Cars	ⅢⅢ ⅢⅢ //	ⅢⅢ ⅢⅢ
Bicycles	////	//
Motorcycles	ⅢⅢ //	///
Vans and lorries	///	ⅢⅢ ⅢⅢ //
Buses and coaches	ⅢⅢ //	///
Others (taxis, etc)	///	
Pedestrians	ⅢⅢ ⅢⅢ ⅢⅢ///	ⅢⅢ ///

Traffic survey

Carry out a traffic survey along the road where you live. Watch the vehicles that pass and fill in the chart. **Make sure you watch from a safe place. Ask an adult whom you know to go with you if you are counting by the side of the road.** On busy roads watch for 10–15 minutes – longer on quieter roads. Watching at different times of day helps. Don't worry if you cannot write down everything.

Finding the energy

We get the energy we need to move from our food. Our muscles and bones work like a machine to move our bodies. This movement is controlled by the brain. A wheelchair helps people who cannot walk. Energy is used up in pushing the wheels by hand.

On your bike

The bicycle makes efficient use of 'people power'. The rider is like an engine providing the power. She eats food for fuel. This gives her the energy to work hard cycling. Extra energy is used to speed up (accelerate).

Air resistance is friction between the air and the bicycle and its rider.

Pushing down on the pedals provides the force that moves the bicycle.

The brakes work by friction. Rubber blocks rub against the wheel and slow down (decelerate) the bicycle.

The chain takes the power to the gears which make the most of the rider's effort. Gears make it easier to climb hills and go faster.

Tyres grip the road because of friction or rubbing. Riding on ice is dangerous because there is very little friction.

Gravity holds the bicycle down to the ground.

1 Karl von Drais invented the first 'hobby-horse' bicycle in 1817. The rider used his legs to push himself along.

2 The pedals of a 'penny farthing' (1870s) were attached to the front wheel. Riders found the large wheel gave a faster and more comfortable ride.

3 This bicycle, from the 1890s, was known as a safety bicycle. A chain took the power from the pedals to the rear wheel. The first safety bicycles had no brakes or gears.

How a steam engine works

1 Fuel is burned on a fire.
2 Water is heated.
3 Hot water turns to steam.
4 Steam fills the cylinder. The steam takes up a lot more space than the water.
5 Steam pressure pushes the piston.
6 Movement of the piston makes the wheels turn.

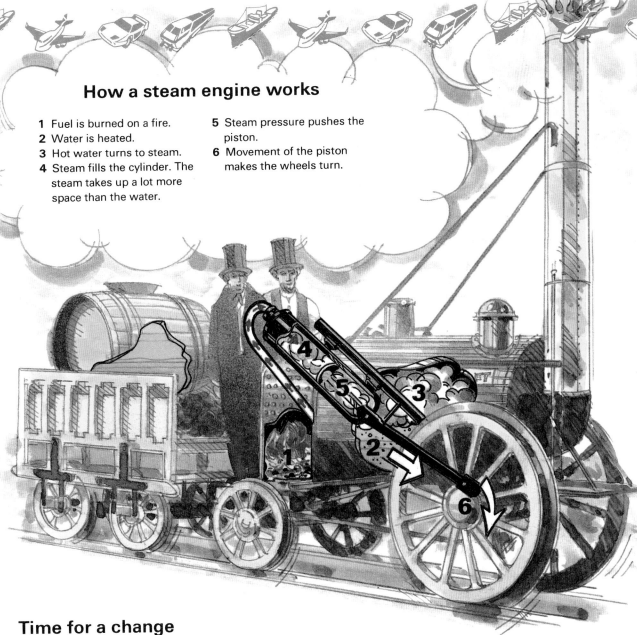

Time for a change

The energy of animals such as oxen and horses can be used to move heavy loads. Animal power is still used in many countries today. However, horses are expensive to buy, feed and look after.

Steam engines were used in factories from the eighteenth century. In 1804, Richard Trevithick showed that a steam engine mounted on a special carriage could be put on rails and used to haul a train. Steam locomotives began to replace horses as the source of power for railways and they are used in some countries today. The strength of machines such as railway locomotives is still measured in 'horse power' (hp).

Like steam engines, motor car and motor bike engines contain pistons. They are forced to move by an explosion made by burning petrol and air. Steam and oil engines have helped make travel possible at higher speeds by land, sea and air. However, all engines pollute the air in some way.

Highway travels

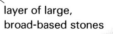

For thousands of years, most people travelled on foot and seldom travelled far from home. Animals could be ridden along tracks called bridleways. Pack horses were used to carry light goods and heavier goods were sent by river or sea. Many old footpaths and bridleways are still used today. Others have been made into roads.

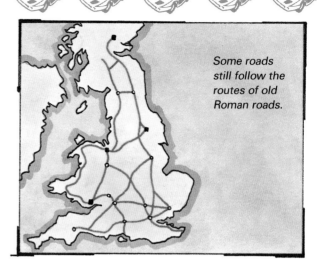

Some roads still follow the routes of old Roman roads.

Many modern roads in Europe follow the routes of old Roman roads. Two thousand years ago, the Roman Empire covered the countries around the Mediterranean Sea and stretched across Europe to Britain. To control their vast empire, the Romans had to be able to move troops and supplies quickly. New roads were built as straight as possible so that journeys would be quick. The roads were usually made from stone and the surface was curved, so that water drained off into ditches on each side. Soldiers marched along the roads and rested at staging posts.

When the Roman Empire came to an end, the road surfaces were no longer repaired. People had to travel on dirt roads, which were often winding, narrow and muddy. Many could only be used in fine weather.

A Telford road in the 1800s

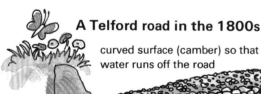

curved surface (camber) so that water runs off the road

drainage ditch

layer of smaller stones

wheels and animals' hooves helped press and crush the stones, filling up any gaps and making the surface waterproof

layer of large, broad-based stones

Thomas Telford
(born 1757; died 1837)

Famous roadbuilders

John McAdam made roads which were cheap to build and easy to look after. Unlike Telford's roads, they had no foundation. Only stones about the size of large marbles were used. The layers of stones were about 15–25cm deep.

John Loudon McAdam
(born 1756; died 1836)

Faster travel

Turnpike roads linked London with many other towns from the 1700s. People had to pay a toll at a tollgate to travel on these roads. For many years local people had to help build the roads. It was backbreaking work.

From 1784, special coaches carried mail and passengers. Mail coaches were fast but expensive to use. The mail was locked in a box and was protected from highway robbers by an armed guard. The mail coaches did not have to stop at tollgates.

Stage coaches

Before the railways were built, stage coaches were used for long journeys. The route was split into stages. Tired horses were replaced by fresh ones in minutes at inns at the end of each stage.

Passengers could sit inside, on top with the luggage, or with the driver. Some could even ride in the rear basket.

The ride was uncomfortable and tiring. Passengers riding on top had to take great care not to fall off. Sometimes passengers had to get off to make it easier for the horses. Imagine what it must have been like in cold weather.

A footman or guard rode on the back of the coach. Most stage coaches had no brakes – they relied on the horses and driver's skill to stop. Candle or oil lamps were used to light their way at night.

Journey from Edinburgh to London

Year	Vehicle	Journey time
1750	Stage coach	10 days
1780	Stage coach	4 days
1830	Mail coach	2 days

Roads and vehicles improved in the eighteenth and nineteenth centuries, but from the mid-1800s, the new railways made journeys even faster. Stage coaches were gradually abandoned.

The open road

During the nineteenth century, people tried to make vehicles that would be cheaper and faster than carriages pulled by horses. Early 'horseless carriages' were steam powered. Later, cars with petrol engines were invented.

These new machines were not popular with everybody. Their speed and noise upset many people. Car tyres damaged the roads and hilly, winding roads made driving difficult. Cars were going to need a new sort of road.

Henry Ford's Model T car

Benz motor car, 1885

16 KPH 10 MPH

70 KPH 43 MPH

4 **14** **30**

1890 1900 1910 1920 1930 19

MILLION MILLIO MILLIO

The first cars

One of the first petrol-engine motor cars was made by Karl Benz of Germany. The car had only three wheels and no roof.

Britain's first cars were not allowed to go very fast. A man holding a red flag had to walk in front! Why do you think this was? Later, cars were allowed to go faster. To celebrate, there was a special outing from London to Brighton. A London to Brighton car run still takes place each year – one hundred years later on.

An American, Henry Ford, built cars cheaply and quickly. His cars were made piece by piece as they passed along a line of men. Each man made only one part of the car. This way of making cars is called a **production line**. Today robots are used on some production lines.

Cars today

Some cars have been very popular for a long time and millions of them have been made. Cars today are very complicated. Computers are used to build and operate them. Modern cars can travel so fast that speed limits are

Lamborghini Diablo (Italy)

325 KPH
202 MPH

Fiat 500 (Italy)

*Volkswagen 'Beetle'
(Germany)*

Austin Mini (UK)

Citroën 2CV (France)

Some of the most popular European cars were
made in vast numbers for many years.

NETHERLANDS
AUTOWEG
100 KPH
62 MPH

GERMANY
AUTOBAHN
130 KPH
80 MPH

UNITED KINGDOM
MOTORWAY
112 KPH
70 MPH

Cars cost a lot of money to build and look after. Even so, there are more today than ever before. Specially built roads help make car journeys quick. For some people, such as doctors or people living in the countryside, a car is essential.

All these cars, however, need a lot of space for roads and car parks. Some towns and major roads have bad traffic jams, and living by a busy road can be smelly, noisy and dangerous.

1950 1960 1970 1980 1990 2000

needed on ordinary roads to make car travel as safe as possible.

Modern roads need to be tough. The surface can be made from concrete, tar or asphalt. Crushed stone is used to make the foundation.

Journey from Edinburgh to London		
Year	Vehicle	Journey time
1930	Motor car	13 hrs 20 mins
1990	Motor car	6 hrs 40 mins

MILLION MILLION
MILLION MILLION
MILLION MILLION
MILLION MILLION
MILLION MILLION
MILLION MILLION
MILLION MILLION
MILLION MILLION
MILLION MILLION
MILLION MILLION

All at sea

The oceans and seas have been used for transport for thousands of years. The dangers of particular oceans are well known and the currents that help sea voyages have been charted. Ships are designed so that they can be used in rough seas, in the dark and in bad weather. Many people, on land and at sea, work to make sea travel safe.

Clippers

Clippers were fast sailing ships that raced across the world carrying cargoes such as tea. The captain of a clipper like this one made sure his ship was properly balanced so that it would go fast. Most clipper routes were taken over by steam ships in the nineteenth century.

Several tall masts supported the sails and rigging.

A good wind provided the energy for sailing ships. Sailing against the wind slowed the ships down.

The bow is the front part of the ship. The rear end is the stern.

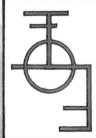

The plimsoll mark and other load lines show if the ship is overloaded or unevenly loaded.

Sailing ships need a keel to keep them upright. Other boats have something heavy in the hull, such as water. This is called ballast.

The hull is the outside body of a ship. The hull of a clipper was long and slim so that it would cut through the water.

10

Where am I?

A ship's navigator must know where the ship is and how to plan its route. Early sailors looked for the sun, clouds and stars. A compass is an instrument with a magnetic needle that shows direction. Chinese sailors used magnetic needles to help them navigate about 900 years ago. Sextants are used to measure the angle of a star or the sun from the horizon. The navigator uses this information to work out the ship's position. Compasses and sextants are still used today, along with radar, computers and satellites.

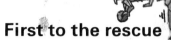

compass

sextant

radar

First to the rescue

Until the twentieth century, local people often went to the rescue of shipwrecked sailors. Today, rescues are organised by the coastguard service. Ships, helicopters and aircraft take part in search and rescue missions. In Britain, volunteers working for the Royal National Lifeboat Institution rescue over a thousand people from the sea every year.

Disaster!

Ships are divided into sections by bulkheads. These are watertight walls which, in an accident, stop water from flooding the whole ship. The luxury liner *Titanic* was designed in this way. It was supposed to be 'unsinkable'.

On 14 April 1912, the *Titanic* struck an iceberg on her maiden voyage across the Atlantic Ocean. Too many sections were flooded and the ship sank with the loss of over 1500 lives. An inquiry found that there were not enough lifeboats on board and that warnings about floating ice had been ignored. Rescue of the survivors was poorly organised.

Lighthouses

One of the first lighthouses was built in Egypt over 2000 years ago. Wood fires marked the coast until the late eighteenth century. Oil was then introduced to provide the light. Coal fires and candles have also been used. Today, automatic lighthouses mark the coast. Each one can be identified by the sequence of its light flashes.

Inland waterways

Before proper roads were built, heavy goods were moved by boat. However, boats could not be used on all rivers. Many were too narrow, too shallow or too fast. From the 1760s, a network of canals was built in Britain, to help solve this problem.

Factories were built near to the new canals. The canals were used to transport materials to the factories and to take away the finished goods. Many businessmen hoped that the better transport provided by the canals would help to make them rich. Eventually, over 6000 km of canals were built.

A boy at work on the Grand Junction Canal in the early 1920s.

Making waterways

A canal is a waterway dug by people. Thousands of men known as 'navvies' (short for 'navigators') built tunnels, embankments, aqueducts and cuttings for the canals. They had only simple tools, such as picks and shovels.

Working the canals

For many years, canal boats were pulled by horses which walked on a towpath alongside the canal. When there was no towpath through a tunnel, the boatmen lay on their backs and pushed off the tunnel walls with their feet to move the boat along.

Eventually, whole families worked the boats. The family lived in a very small cabin. Children worked the locks and led the horses. Later, canal boats were powered by engines.

How a lock works

Rivers flow gradually downwards but canals have to be kept on the level. Locks were built so that boats could move from one height to another.

1 The boat has to move to a higher level of the canal.

2 The sluice gates are opened. Water pours out of the lock, until the water reaches the same level as the boat.

3 The lock gates are opened. The boat moves into the lock and the gates are closed.

4 The sluice gates of the second gate are opened. The water level in the lock rises.

5 When the water in the lock reaches the higher level, the second gates are opened and the boat moves along the canal.

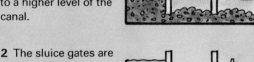

Today's canals

When the railways were built, canals became less popular. Rail transport was faster and cheaper. Many disused canals became broken down and overgrown. Some canals in Britain have been restored by volunteers, so that people can visit them and enjoy travelling by canal boat. Today, there are over 5600 km of canals and navigable rivers in Britain. Wider canals, such as those in Europe, are used by larger boats to move heavy goods cheaply. Rivers and lakes are used more than canals in other parts of the world.

Ship canals

Large canals are used by ships to reach inland ports, or to link oceans and seas. The Manchester Ship Canal was opened in 1894 so that ships could reach Manchester from the River Mersey. In North America, ships travel thousands of kilometres inland, from the Atlantic Ocean to the Great Lakes, along the St Lawrence River, using special locks.

Suez Canal

Africa

The largest ship canal is the Suez Canal. It was opened in 1869 and links the Mediterranean and Red Seas. It is a useful short cut and saves a long journey around Africa.

Some English narrowboats measure over 21 m long and 2 m wide.

Wide barges use rivers and broad canals. In France, freight barges can be 35 m long and nearly 5 m wide.

The largest ocean-going ship to use the Suez Canal was over 300 m long and almost 60 m wide.

The train now departing

Rolling a vehicle along smooth rails makes it easier to move. Horses pulled mining wagons on rails hundreds of years ago. Steam locomotives were first used to haul passenger trains in 1825 on the Stockton and Darlington Railway. The cities of Liverpool and Manchester were joined by a railway in 1830. Within twenty years railways were built all over Europe and America.

The railway builders

The Liverpool and Manchester Railway was designed by George Stephenson. It had to go up steep slopes and across boggy ground. Cuttings and tunnels were blasted through the rock. The loose rock was used to make embankments. Over sixty bridges had to be built. Heather and wood were laid across bogs to stop the railway sinking.

William Powell Frith's 'The Railway Station' (1863).

Railway travel was cheaper, faster and more comfortable than stage coaches and canals. It took some people a while to get used to it.

Here are some reports of injuries to early train travellers:

Imagine what life must have been like for the thousands of men who built the first railways. Like the canal builders, they were known as navvies. They lived in squalid camps alongside the railway. The tools they used were very simple – picks and shovels – and horses were used to pull the wagons which took away the broken rock.

fell out of a third-class carriage while pushing and jostling with a friend

skull broken, riding on the top of the carriage, came in collision with bridge

run over while lying asleep on the line

injured, jumped out after his hat

The Channel Tunnel

Building a bridge or tunnel between France and Britain is an old idea. The first unsuccessful attempt to build a tunnel was in 1877. Over a hundred years later, both countries agreed to try again.

Once the engineers had found out what the rock beneath the Channel was like, they used special boring machines, like giant drills, to dig tunnels through the rock. The tunnels are lined with concrete or iron. Laser beams were used to make sure the tunnels were straight. The nineteenth-century navvies would be amazed to see the computers, conveyor belts and electric railway used to build the tunnel.

The picture shows the layout of the Channel Tunnel, which is 50 km (31 miles) long. Special terminals are needed to load vehicles on to the 160 kph electric trains.

High-speed trains

Today, trains travel at great speed, often over long distances – sometimes across whole continents.

The 'Bullet' trains of Japan can travel at speeds up to 275 kph (over 170 mph) on special track.

'TGV' trains connect many towns and cities in France. One of these trains reached a speed of 380 kph (236 mph) – a world record – in 1981.

High fliers

For thousands of years people have dreamed of being able to fly. At first, they tried to copy the birds – but they were unsuccessful. Eventually, hot air got the first pilots off the ground. Since then, all sorts of flying machines have been invented.

Lighter than air

Two French brothers, Joseph and Etienne de Montgolfier, invented the first hot-air balloon in 1783. Their first passengers were a duck, a sheep and a cock! People were amazed.

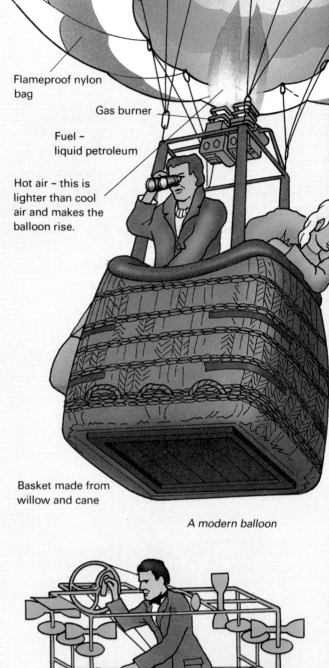

Flameproof nylon bag

Gas burner

Fuel – liquid petroleum

Hot air – this is lighter than cool air and makes the balloon rise.

Basket made from willow and cane

A modern balloon

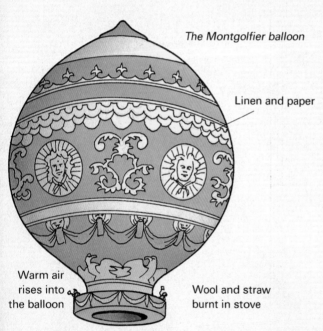

The Montgolfier balloon

Linen and paper

Warm air rises into the balloon

Wool and straw burnt in stove

' . . . *raising the fire once more, we turned south . . . and when extinguishing the flame, the balloon came down spent and empty.* '
(The Marquis d'Arlandes, one of the first people to fly in a hot-air balloon, Paris, 1783)

This flying machine was invented in 1885 by an American, Doctor Ayres. It would have been difficult to fly had it worked.

Up, up and away

The first airship was invented in 1852. Unlike a balloon, which drifts in the wind, it had a steam engine and a propeller to guide it through the air. It was filled with hydrogen gas, which is lighter than air, but very explosive. Zeppelin airships were made in Germany from 1900. They were used for passengers and, during the First World War, for dropping bombs. In 1929, the *Graf Zeppelin* flew round the world.

'I heard a crash and . . . explosions. There were blinding flashes . . . and the next thing I knew was that the ship was on fire.'

(A survivor from the crash of airship *R101*, France, 1930)

In 1930, the British airship *R101* crashed in France, killing 48 people. Seven years later, the German airship *Hindenburg* (left) burst into flames in the USA, bringing the age of passenger airships to an end.

The Flyer

By this time, aeroplanes were carrying passengers at greater speeds than the airships. Orville and Wilbur Wright had made the first powered flight in 'The Flyer' in 1903. 'The Flyer' flew about 36 m (120 ft), at a height of around 3 m above the ground. Planes like this, with two wings, are called biplanes.

How planes fly

Lift: air rushes over the top of the wing and pushes from below, lifting the plane.

Thrust: the propeller pulls the plane through the air.

Drag: the air pushes against the plane as it flies forward.

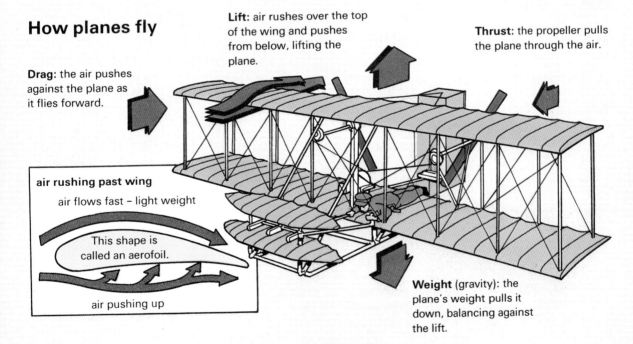

air rushing past wing

air flows fast – light weight

This shape is called an aerofoil.

air pushing up

Weight (gravity): the plane's weight pulls it down, balancing against the lift.

The aeroplane age

Air travel today is fast but expensive. Aircraft are used to carry freight, such as fresh food and mail. Many far-away places are now popular holiday resorts, because people can fly to them quickly. Air transport is essential for people living in remote areas. In Australia, for example, small planes are used to carry doctors and medical equipment to isolated places.

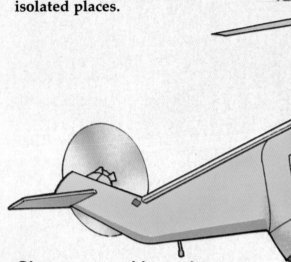

Choppers and jump jets

Helicopters and jump jets are known as vertical take-off and landing aircraft. Being able to land and take off vertically is useful when there is no room for a long runway – on a ship, for example.

Helicopters can hover in the same spot while rescuing people from the sea.

Flying a helicopter

A helicopter is lifted upwards by its spinning rotor blades.

Hovering

The helicopter hovers in one spot when the rotor blades are level and spinning fast.

Flying forwards

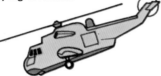

The rotor blades are tilted down at the front. The air is pushed back and the helicopter moves forward.

Flying backwards

The rotor blades are tilted back. Air is pulled in front of the helicopter and it moves backwards.

Faster and further

Fighting aircraft that could fly higher and faster than ever before were used at the end of the Second World War.

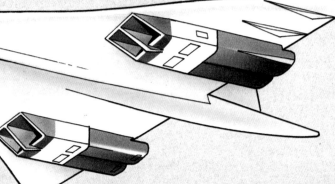

These were jet propelled. Jet engines thrust an aircraft forward by sucking in air and forcing it out at great speed. The fastest jet airliner in the world is Concorde. It can fly at 2333 kph (1450 mph) – faster than the speed of sound. Military jets can fly at even greater speeds.

The flightdeck of a modern aeroplane is crammed with electronics. Between take-off and landing, the plane is controlled automatically, but the pilots check the instruments all the time.

Jump jets

A Harrier jump jet lands and takes off vertically.

To take off, nozzles direct the thrust from the engines downwards.

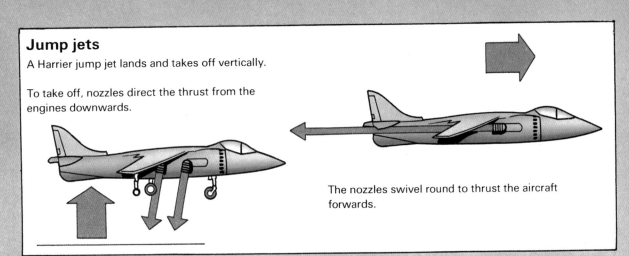

The nozzles swivel round to thrust the aircraft forwards.

Town and country

Towns used to be smaller than they are today. Most people walked everywhere. With better transport, people, especially the most wealthy, were able to travel further and more quickly. Towns spread out and grew along roads and railways. New homes were built in the countryside, on the edges of towns. These areas are called suburbs. In Britain, new towns such as Milton Keynes have been designed for the age of the motor car.

Offices, large shops and railway terminals are usually in the centres of towns. People travel (commute) from the suburbs to the town centres to work. Many people travel by car. Others use public transport – buses, trains and trams. Some travel by bike. Traffic jams build up in the mornings, when everyone is going to work, and again in the evenings, as they travel home. These busy times are called rush hours.

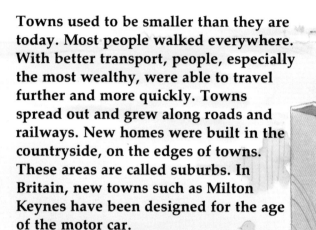
Car parks at the edge of the town. People travel into the centre by public transport.

In the country
Villages in the countryside may be far apart and journeys to schools and shops can take a long time. Car owners can travel when they like. Young people and the elderly may have to rely on public transport – and there may be only two buses each day. Library and shop vans go from village to village for people who have no transport. Minibuses are used in some areas too.

Rapid transit systems move a lot of people very quickly.

Solving the problems

Some people think the answer to traffic problems in towns is to build better roads and more car parks. Others think cars should be kept out of towns and public transport made more efficient. New technology can be used to help traffic flow more smoothly. The picture shows some ways of solving traffic problems in towns.

Offices, factories and shopping centres away from the town centre.

Subways, bridges and elevated skywalks make it easier for pedestrians to cross roads.

Pedestrian-only shopping areas make walking in towns more pleasant.

Cycleways make it easier and safer for cyclists to travel around the town centre.

People start and finish work at different times.

No cars in the town centre, so buses and trams do not get stuck in traffic jams.

'Plenty of room on top!'

This used to be a familiar cry from the bus conductor! Sitting on the top deck of an early double-deck bus must have been good fun when the weather was fine. When it rained, it was more comfortable to sit inside, down below.

The first horse-drawn 'omnibus' service began in France over 150 years ago. Services began in London soon after. A journey by omnibus saved the time and effort of walking – if you could afford it. At first, the new service was too expensive for many people, yet the word 'omnibus' means 'for all'!

The bus conductor gives out tickets and helps people on and off the bus. Today, many buses do not have conductors. Passengers pay the driver as they get on. Sometimes computers are used to print the tickets.

All change
These London buses are all mixed up. Can you put them in the order they were made – starting with the oldest and ending with the most modern?

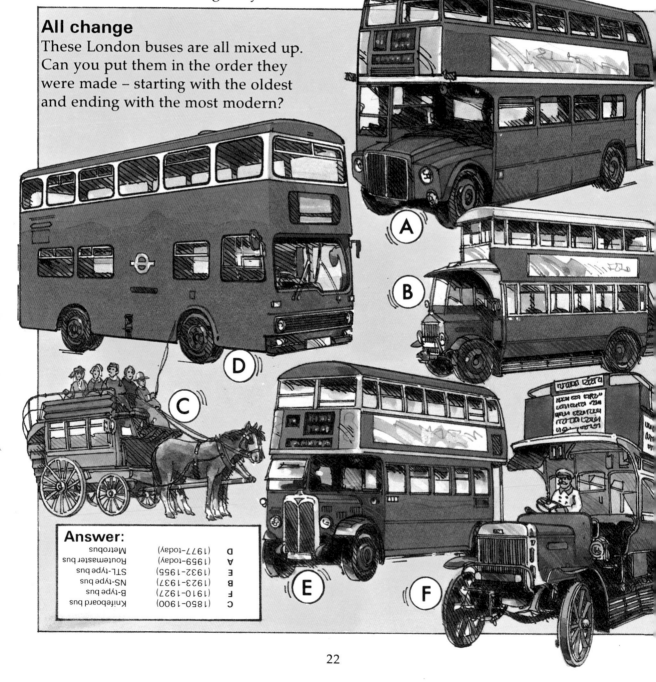

Answer:

C	(1850–1900) Knifeboard bus
F	(1910–1927) B-type bus
B	(1923–1937) NS-type bus
E	(1932–1955) STL-type bus
A	(1959–today) Routemaster bus
D	(1977–today) Metrobus

Travelling by bus

Today, millions of people all over the world go by bus. Buses run to a timetable on a fixed route. In towns, they make frequent stops. Others provide express services, linking towns and cities.

A bus must be safe, reliable and easy to operate. It must also be big enough to carry many passengers and their luggage and easy to get on and off. It has to show where it is going too! Some buses are specially designed to do a particular job.

Some buses in Bangladesh have strengthened roofs, to carry the weight of passengers and luggage.

Articulated buses can be used to carry many people in busy town centres.

Buses with electric lifts can be used more easily by disabled people.

In the USA, Greyhound coaches travel long distances at high speeds. Many have air conditioning, toilets, refreshments and videos.

The picture shows a modern trolley bus in Marseilles. Electric trolley buses were first used in Germany in 1901. Can you think why electric vehicles are even more popular today?

Back on track

Tramways in towns, or 'street railways', are an American invention. Trams work rather like a bus on a track – they run on smooth metal rails set into the road.

Britain's first street trams were tried out in Birkenhead and were pulled by horses. The smooth rails made it easier for horses to pull the trams, so they could carry 50 passengers. The omnibus had to be pulled along bumpy cobbled streets and could carry only half this number of passengers. More people could afford the cheap tram fares and many travelled by tram to work.

Later, because the horses were so expensive to buy and look after, many cities built electric tramways. Electricity passed along wires over the tracks or through a slot in the road.

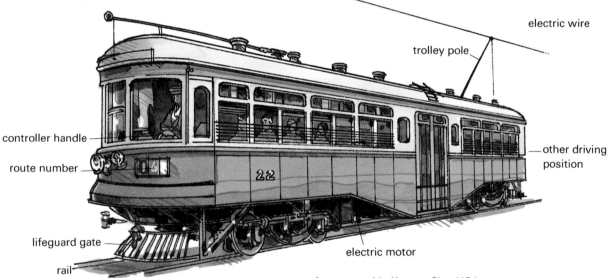

A tram used in Kansas City, USA, in the early twentieth century.

Labels: electric wire, trolley pole, controller handle, route number, other driving position, lifeguard gate, rail, electric motor, 22

Trams today

Trams were not popular with everybody. Can you think why some wealthy people did not want trams in their neighbourhood? Some people thought trams made traffic jams worse. They were expensive to build too.

In Britain, electric trolleybuses and motor buses eventually replaced the trams – except in the seaside town Blackpool, where there are still electric trams. The trams do not pollute the air and they can move quickly.

Some towns are now building modern tramways – or are thinking of doing so. Some people believe trams will help improve transport systems in our cities. Can you think of any problems with trams?

Trams or light rail vehicles are used in many countries around the world. At Hanover, in Germany, the track has been laid in the middle of a dual carriageway – away from other traffic. Special zebra-crossings help passengers reach the tram stop.

'Any more fares, please?'
Imagine doing the job of a tram conductor. It is midday (12.00) on 18 October 1920.

How often do trams run into town first thing in the morning, please?

(answer: every 15 minutes)

Can you tell me what time the last tram leaves the town hall, please?

(answer: 23.38/ 11.38 pm)

How much is the fare for two children and one adult from the 'Coach and Horses' to the Town Hall, please?

(answer: six stages, off peak. One adult at two pennies, two children at 1½ pennies each, makes five pennies altogether!)

How much is a workman's ticket from the depot to the town hall, please?

(answer: eight fare stages – two pennies.)

Tram routes were divided into sections called fare stages. The price of a journey depended on how many stages were travelled.

The passenger who bought this ticket paid a one penny fare. He or she was travelling towards the town centre (up). The conductor punched a hole in the ticket to show how far the passenger could travel. The paper punched from the tickets could be counted to check the conductor's takings.

TICKET NUMBER 9858

THE ELECTRIC TRAM COMPANY — ONE PENNY 1d

UP TO FARE STAGE	DOWN TO FARE STAGE
Depot to Brunswick Street	Town Hall to Central Library
St. Anne's Church to Baker Street	Railway Station to Alderson Road
"Coach and Horses" to Playing Field	High Street to Department Store
Rubber factory to Cross Street	Bridge Lane to Town Gate
Town Gate to Bridge Lane	Cross Street to Rubber factory
Department Store to High Street	Playing Field to "Coach and Horses"
Alderson Road to Railway Station	Baker Street to St. Anne's Church
Central Library to Town Hall	Brunswick Street to Depot

FARES

NUMBER OF STAGES TRAVELLED	1	2	3	4	5	6	7	8
ORDINARY PRICE (pennies)	1	1	2	2	3	3	4	4
CHILDREN (pennies)	1	1	1	1	1½	1½	2	2
WORKMANS (only before 08·00 and after 18·00) pennies	½	½	1	1	1½	1½	2	2
OFF PEAK (after 10·00 and before 18·00)	1	1	2	2	2	2	2	2
SEAT WILL DAY TICKET	1/- one Shilling							

1d   1½d   2d   3d   4d   1/-

DIRECTION : UP				
DEPOT	BAKER STREET	CROSS STREET	HIGH STREET	TOWN HALL
05·00	05·06	05·12	05·20	05·28
05·15	05·21	05·27	05·35	05·43
05·30	05·36	05·42	05·50	05·58
05·45	05·51	05·57	06·05	06·13
06·00	06·06	06·12	06·20	06·28

LAST TRAMS	DEPOT	TOWN HALL	DEPOT
UP	23·00	23·28	–
DOWN	–	23·38	00·06

CLUN C. PRIMARY CLYNE

Under and over

Rapid transit or metro trains run on tracks, often underground or raised above the streets. Transport like this helps to reduce traffic jams in busy town streets. The trains move a lot of people very quickly.

Steam and sardines

The first underground railway was London's Metropolitan Railway, opened in 1863. The tunnels were built by covering over a trench, usually along the route of a road. This was called 'cut and cover'. Steam locomotives filled the tunnels with steam and smoke.

There are now more than 60 rapid transit railways in cities all over the world. New York, in the USA, had an elevated railway and now has an underground railway called the Subway. Buenos Aires (Argentina), Tokyo (Japan), Melbourne (Australia) and Cairo (Egypt) all have rapid transit railways.

Escaping the traffic jams: a London Underground poster from the 1920s.

Eight-year-old Peter Robinson took just over 18 hours and 41 minutes to tour all London Underground's stations in 1986.

The City and South London Railway was much deeper. From the bottom of a deep shaft the tunnels were dug by hand and lined with rings of iron to make a 'tube'. The railway opened in 1890 and, for the first time, used electric locomotives. It was nicknamed the 'sardine box railway'.

The SkyTrain in Vancouver, Canada. It was opened in 1986, to improve the city's transport system without making more roads. The trains have no drivers – they are controlled by computers. SkyTrains run on elevated lines, on the surface and underground.

New York's Subway is the metro system with the most stations. There are over 460 of them.

ticket gates

emergency equipment

street entrance

emergency stairs

electric escalator

(running) tunnel

electrified tracks

passageway

elevated railway

signals

platform

The busiest metro system is in Moscow, in the USSR. Just over three billion passengers travel on it each year.

deep tube railway

Taxi!

Not everybody has a car or can drive. Roads are busy and finding a parking space can be difficult. More and more people are using taxis instead of cars.

Travelling by taxi is like travelling by car. A fare has to be paid to the driver for taking you where you want to go. There is no timetable – you can usually hire a taxi whenever you need one. Unlike buses, taxis can go almost anywhere, taking you from door to door quickly and safely. However, a taxi ride is more expensive than a journey by bus or train. Taxis are useful for people who are elderly, disabled or have a lot of luggage. Many people use them to get to an airport, railway or bus station.

Taxi drivers have to train hard. Many 'cabbies' have to pass a test to show that they know the roads and important buildings in their local area. A good memory helps.

Dial-a-ride minibuses also work like taxis. People can telephone to fix up their journey. The minibus then collects a group of people and takes them where they want to go. Dial-a-ride minibuses are mostly used by elderly and disabled people.

New York's yellow cabs carry about one million people each day.

In the poorer parts of some cities, such as Caracas in South America, and Mexico City in Central America, people often share makeshift taxis made from vans called jitneys.

Motor cabs like this Austin taxi have been used in London since 1958. They can also be seen in many other cities in Britain.

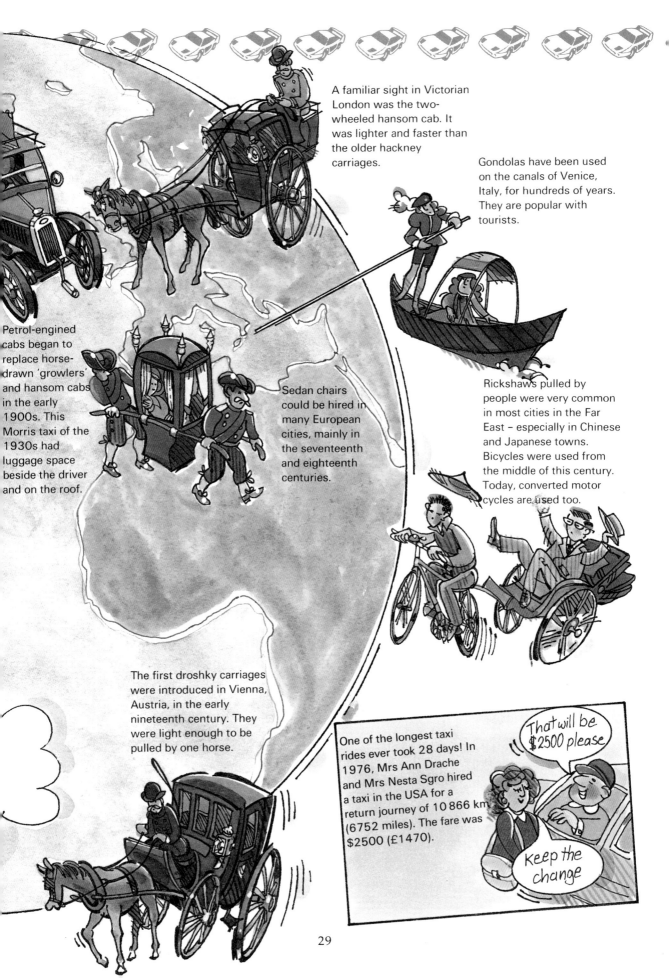

A familiar sight in Victorian London was the two-wheeled hansom cab. It was lighter and faster than the older hackney carriages.

Gondolas have been used on the canals of Venice, Italy, for hundreds of years. They are popular with tourists.

Petrol-engined cabs began to replace horse-drawn 'growlers' and hansom cabs in the early 1900s. This Morris taxi of the 1930s had luggage space beside the driver and on the roof.

Sedan chairs could be hired in many European cities, mainly in the seventeenth and eighteenth centuries.

Rickshaws pulled by people were very common in most cities in the Far East – especially in Chinese and Japanese towns. Bicycles were used from the middle of this century. Today, converted motor cycles are used too.

The first droshky carriages were introduced in Vienna, Austria, in the early nineteenth century. They were light enough to be pulled by one horse.

One of the longest taxi rides ever took 28 days! In 1976, Mrs Ann Drache and Mrs Nesta Sgro hired a taxi in the USA for a return journey of 10 866 km (6752 miles). The fare was $2500 (£1470).

That will be $2500 please

Keep the change

Delivering the goods

Next time you have a meal, think about how the food arrived in your home. It might have been brought from far away by ship, or from a nearby factory, and delivered by road to your local shops. Transporting goods such as food is called freight transport.

Some foods, like milk, have to be transported quickly because they soon go bad. Special trucks are used to transport animals to market. Foods such as grain are moved in bulk by cargo ships. Coal is moved on long freight trains or barges.

Milk on the move

Milk is an important food. Large amounts of it have to be moved quickly from the farms where it is produced to factories, where it is put into bottles and cartons, and then to people's homes.

Hand carts like this one were used to deliver milk to people's homes in the 1890s.

By the late nineteenth century, milk was transported to most cities by train. The churns were taken from farms to the railway station by horse and cart. Later, milk churns were transported by lorry.

In Britain, electric milk floats are used to deliver bottles and cartons of milk to people's homes.

Today, most milk in Britain is transported by road in refrigerated tankers.

Road trains

Very large trucks are called juggernauts. They help save money, because one truck can move a lot of goods, but they are noisy. Enormous road trains are used in countries such as Australia and the USA. They move quickly and carry large loads over very long distances. They are articulated, which means a power unit, or 'tractor', as it is known, is used to tow several trailers joined together. This makes it easier to go round bends.

This pie chart shows the proportion of freight moved by lorry, train, boat and pipe in the UK.

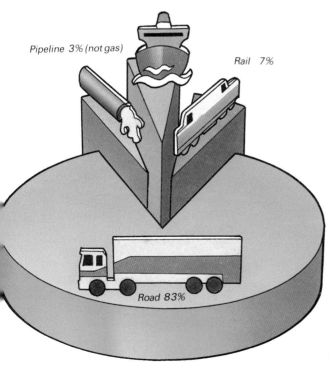

Water 7% (inland and coastal)

Pipeline 3% (not gas)

Rail 7%

Road 83%

Past and present

At first, rivers were used to move heavy goods. When better roads were built, carts became more important. From the eighteenth century, canals were used for freight transport, until the arrival of the faster, cheaper railway system in the mid-nineteenth century.

Today, a lot of freight is moved in steel containers loaded on to lorries, ships and trains. Large tankers carry oil and are often loaded and unloaded offshore by underwater pipes. Pipelines move oil, gas and water over thousands of kilometres. Air transport is fast but expensive. Water transport is cheaper but slow. Railways are quick but, unlike roads, they cannot link every town and village.

Source: 1991 Annual Abstract of Statistics, Central Statistical Office.

On the level

Imagine cycling over a hill. Going up would be difficult. Gravity would make riding down easier – as long as you had good brakes! If you could ride your bicycle round the hill and keep on the level it would make your journey easier but longer. A tunnel under the hill would make the ride easy and quick.

Crossing mountains and deep valleys with roads or railways can be difficult. Tunnels and bridges help keep journeys short, quick and easy, but they are expensive and often dangerous to build. Sometimes a toll charge has to be paid to use them. They help save the energy which would be used getting up a hill or going the long way round.

In parts of Australia where the land is very flat, long trains run on straight track with few gradients.

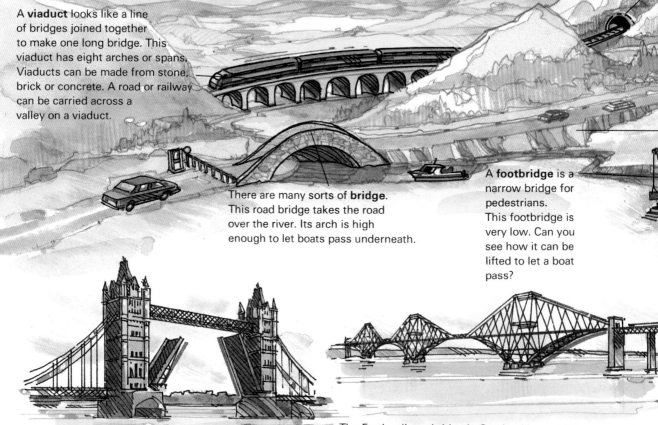

A **viaduct** looks like a line of bridges joined together to make one long bridge. This viaduct has eight arches or spans. Viaducts can be made from stone, brick or concrete. A road or railway can be carried across a valley on a viaduct.

There are many sorts of **bridge**. This road bridge takes the road over the river. Its arch is high enough to let boats pass underneath.

A **footbridge** is a narrow bridge for pedestrians. This footbridge is very low. Can you see how it can be lifted to let a boat pass?

Tower Bridge in London is a **bascule** bridge. The two halves of the deck can be lifted to let ships pass.

The Forth railway bridge in Scotland is a **cantilever** bridge made from steel. It was opened in 1890. A cantilever is a beam supported by only one pier.

Transport in the landscape

This **tunnel** takes the railway underground through the mountain. Tunnels can be dug by hand or with machines. Explosives are used to loosen the rock.

A **cutting** is a steep-sided trench dug out of the rock.

An **embankment** is a bank of earth or rock. Sometimes the rock dug from a cutting is piled up to make an embankment.

Building bridges

1 Make two piers from books or cardboard boxes. Place them 40 cm apart. This distance is called the span. Bridge the gap with a piece of cardboard about 50 cm long. This is called the deck.

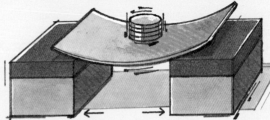

2 Test the strength of this simple bridge. You will need some small weights – 10p coins will do. How many weights do you think the bridge will hold? Place one weight at a time in the centre of the deck until the bridge collapses. Remember how many weights you use.

3 Try the test again but this time shorten the span by moving the piers closer together.

4 Replace the deck.

5 Take a second piece of card about the same size and gently bend it to make an arch. Place the arch between the piers so that it just touches the deck. You will have to shorten the span of the bridge by bringing the piers closer together.

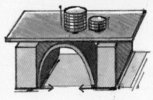

6 Test the strength of this bridge using the weights. How many weights do you think the bridge will support?

Try other ways to make a strong bridge.

The Golden Gate bridge in San Francisco, USA, is a **suspension** bridge. Steel cables hang from two towers. The deck is hung or suspended from the cables.

The first iron road bridge was opened in 1779. This **arch** bridge was built across the River Severn in Shropshire. The nearby town is called Ironbridge.

Transport specials

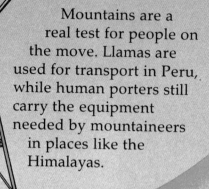

The shape of the land is different from place to place. There are different climates around the world too. Special sorts of transport are needed for these environments.

Mountains are a real test for people on the move. Llamas are used for transport in Peru, while human porters still carry the equipment needed by mountaineers in places like the Himalayas.

Mountain railways need special track to make sure the trains cannot run away. Cable cars are popular in mountainous ski resorts, where they carry people to the top of the ski runs.

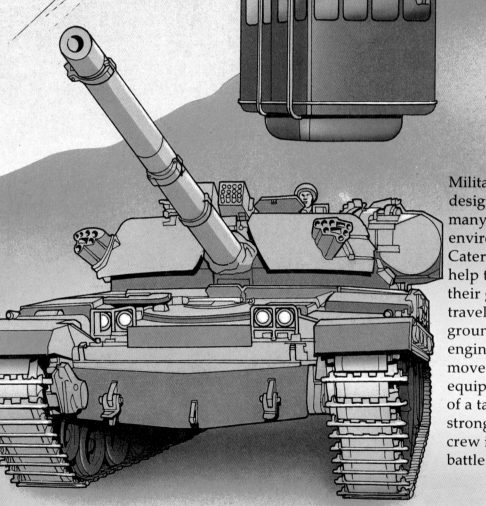

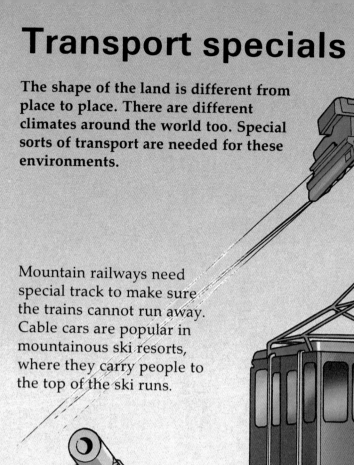

Military transport is designed for use in many difficult environments. Caterpillar tracks help tanks to keep their grip as they travel over rough ground. A powerful engine is needed to move the heavy equipment. The body of a tank is very strong, to protect the crew inside during a battle.

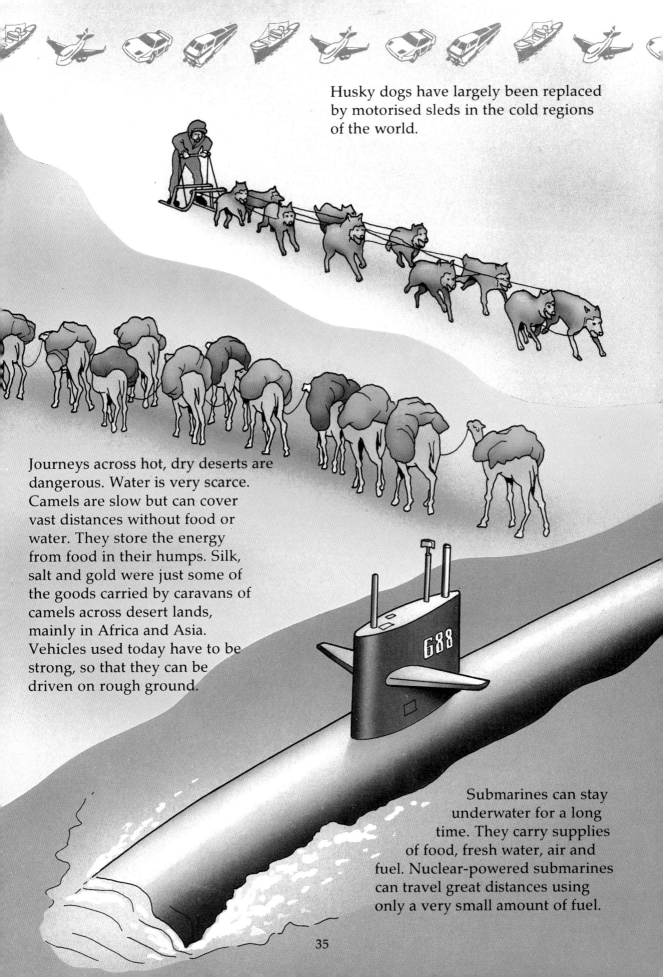

Husky dogs have largely been replaced by motorised sleds in the cold regions of the world.

Journeys across hot, dry deserts are dangerous. Water is very scarce. Camels are slow but can cover vast distances without food or water. They store the energy from food in their humps. Silk, salt and gold were just some of the goods carried by caravans of camels across desert lands, mainly in Africa and Asia. Vehicles used today have to be strong, so that they can be driven on rough ground.

Submarines can stay underwater for a long time. They carry supplies of food, fresh water, air and fuel. Nuclear-powered submarines can travel great distances using only a very small amount of fuel.

Red for danger

Safety when travelling is very important. On modern roads, traffic lights help to prevent drivers from colliding. Railway signals do a similar job, keeping trains a safe distance apart and running on time. They show drivers when to slow down or stop and they also show which route has been set.

Railway signals

In the early days, railway policemen let trains go at set times. Drivers just hoped the way ahead was clear. At least trains did not go very fast then. Later, signalmen sent messages to each other to show where each train was. They used the electric telegraph to do this.

A main-line signal box in the 1940s.

Signal boxes

Signals are controlled from a signal box and each box controls a section of the line. Special care is taken when trains move in both directions on one track. In modern signal boxes, the levers that worked the points and signals have been replaced by push buttons. An electronic map shows the movement of each train. Computers are also used. Fewer signal boxes are needed now.

Stop and go

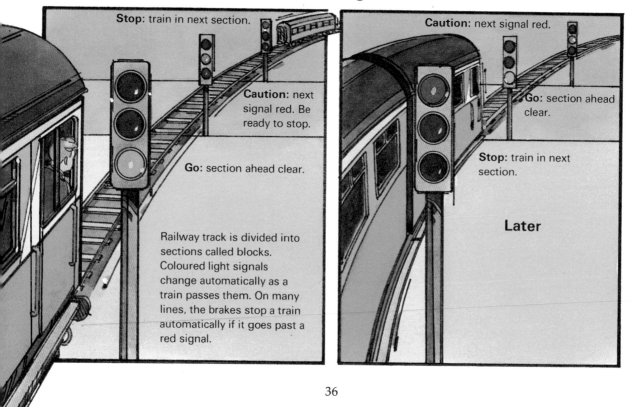

Stop: train in next section.

Caution: next signal red. Be ready to stop.

Go: section ahead clear.

Railway track is divided into sections called blocks. Coloured light signals change automatically as a train passes them. On many lines, the brakes stop a train automatically if it goes past a red signal.

Caution: next signal red.

Go: section ahead clear.

Stop: train in next section.

Later

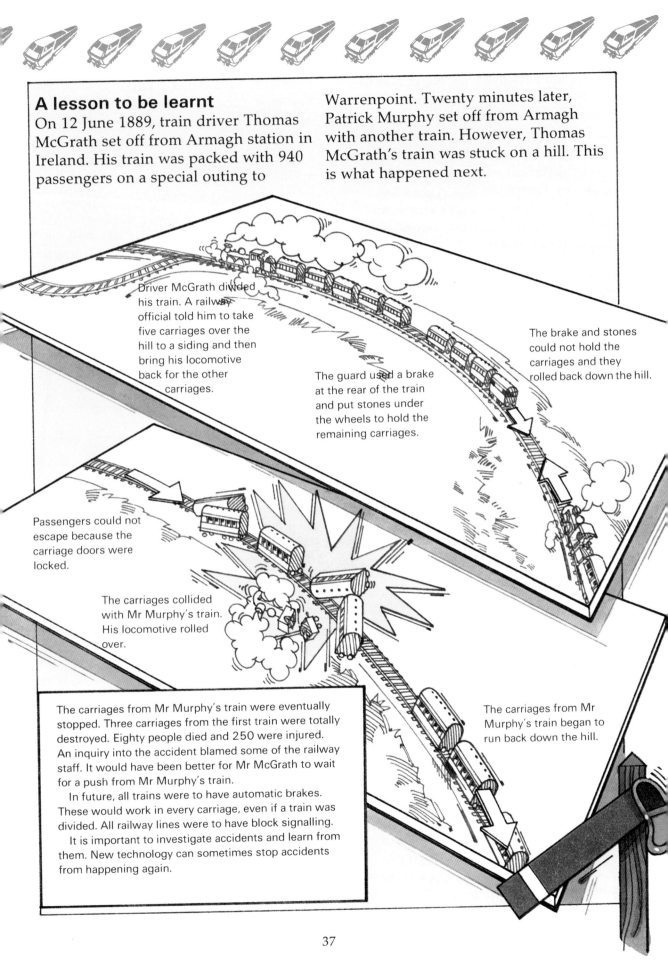

A lesson to be learnt

On 12 June 1889, train driver Thomas McGrath set off from Armagh station in Ireland. His train was packed with 940 passengers on a special outing to Warrenpoint. Twenty minutes later, Patrick Murphy set off from Armagh with another train. However, Thomas McGrath's train was stuck on a hill. This is what happened next.

Driver McGrath divided his train. A railway official told him to take five carriages over the hill to a siding and then bring his locomotive back for the other carriages.

The guard used a brake at the rear of the train and put stones under the wheels to hold the remaining carriages.

The brake and stones could not hold the carriages and they rolled back down the hill.

Passengers could not escape because the carriage doors were locked.

The carriages collided with Mr Murphy's train. His locomotive rolled over.

The carriages from Mr Murphy's train began to run back down the hill.

The carriages from Mr Murphy's train were eventually stopped. Three carriages from the first train were totally destroyed. Eighty people died and 250 were injured. An inquiry into the accident blamed some of the railway staff. It would have been better for Mr McGrath to wait for a push from Mr Murphy's train.

In future, all trains were to have automatic brakes. These would work in every carriage, even if a train was divided. All railway lines were to have block signalling.

It is important to investigate accidents and learn from them. New technology can sometimes stop accidents from happening again.

Networks and maps

Transport networks are the routes of roads, railway tracks and canals. There are many other types of transport network. Some are very simple, others are very complex. In big cities there are lots of different networks – roads and railways, footpaths and cycle ways. Then there are gas, water and sewer pipes, electricity and telephone cables. These are vital networks too!

Finding the best route

The way a transport network looks depends on where the routes go. Roads and railways are built where they are for a reason, for example, to link towns or to link a coal mine to a port. A transport route is usually the shortest distance between places.

Look at the map. Choose the best route for a railway between Northtown and Southside.

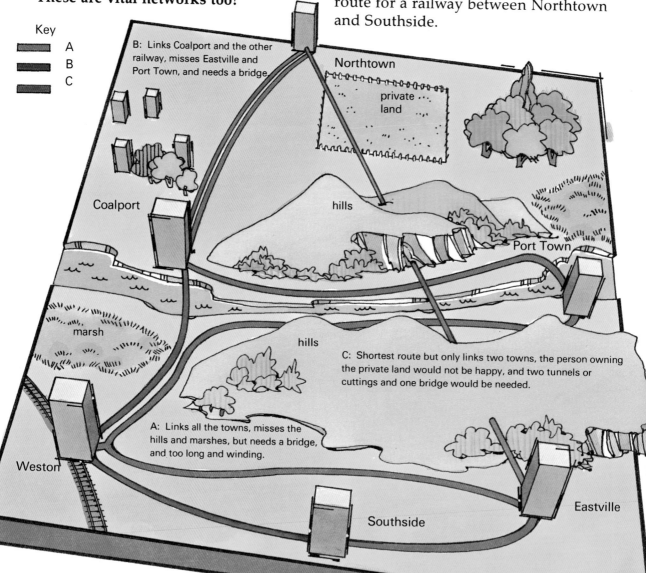

Key

A

B

C

B: Links Coalport and the other railway, misses Eastville and Port Town, and needs a bridge.

Northtown

private land

hills

Coalport

hills

Port Town

C: Shortest route but only links two towns, the person owning the private land would not be happy, and two tunnels or cuttings and one bridge would be needed.

marsh

hills

A: Links all the towns, misses the hills and marshes, but needs a bridge, and too long and winding.

Weston

Eastville

Southside

Routes cannot go everywhere. Hills, lakes and buildings get in the way. People may object to having a road or railway built near them. The routes that are chosen have to be the best that can be afforded.

Changing networks

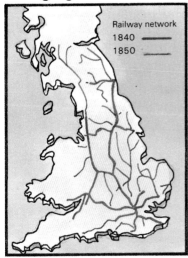

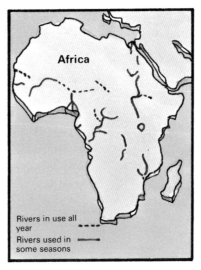

Railway network
1840 ——
1850 ——

Africa

Rivers in use all
year ‑‑‑‑
Rivers used in
some seasons ——

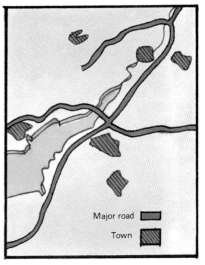

Major road
Town

A transport network may change over the years. New routes may be added, others taken away.

The amount of water in a river changes. In dry months it might be too shallow for boats to use.

Some river mouths are very wide. Bridges can sometimes be built to save a long journey round the river estuary.

Bird's-eye view

Roads join to make a junction. Bridges let roads and railways cross. Can you think of any other ways in which transport routes cross each other? Look at the joins and cross-overs in this aerial photo, taken looking down from an aeroplane.

Making sense of it

Maps help people to understand transport networks and find their way around. They can plan their journey and the route they must take. There are many different kinds of transport map. This one helps people to find their way around the London Underground network.

The end of the line

An airport is a transport terminal – a place where journeys begin and end. Seaports, railway stations and bus stations are all transport terminals. They are interchanges too, where people change from one sort of transport to another.

Two of the world's biggest airports are Chicago O'Hare in the USA and London Heathrow. About 50 000 people work at Heathrow. Aircraft are refuelled, freight is loaded and unloaded and people wait for their flights in restaurants and departure lounges. Busy airports can be noisy – many people do not want new and bigger airports to be built.

hotel

aircraft hangars

main road

fuel stores

control tower

freight warehouses

rail link

car parks

taxi rank

baggage handling

customs and immigration

observation balcony

servicing vehicles

emergency services

Choosing the best sites

Airports need a lot of flat land, away from hills and mountains. Areas that get a lot of snow, fog and high winds are bad sites for airports, as they have to be closed in very bad weather. An airport also has to have good road and rail links, so that passengers can travel to and from it easily. Airport workers need a nearby town to live in.

Seaports

Freight is usually moved over long distances by ships. The world's largest seaport is Rotterdam-Europoort, in the Netherlands (below). Ports like this need deep water, shelter from storms and space for warehouses. Some ports, in the USSR, for example, cannot be used in the winter because of ice.

London was once the busiest seaport in the world. Small boats ferried goods to and from ships moored in the River Thames. In the nineteenth century, docks were built to make loading and unloading easier. However, ships became too large for the docks. A new container port was built at Tilbury and the old London docks closed down.

Containers are packed with goods in factories and taken to the port by train or lorry. Special cranes load the containers on to the ship, with computers making sure that the heaviest containers are loaded first. Goods can be loaded faster and more cheaply than at the old docks. Fewer dock workers are needed to do the job.

apron

taxiing runway

take-off and landing runway

Transport and the environment

Different landscapes make transport easy or difficult. Solid, level ground makes transport easy. Valleys can make good routes. Mountains get in the way. Snow, ice and fog make travel dangerous and journeys can be made uncomfortable by heat, cold and rain. Deserts, forests and marshes are difficult to cross. Floods, earthquakes and avalanches can make some transport routes dangerous.

Damaging the landscape

Transport can have a bad effect on the landscape too. In the picture below, a lot of harm is being done to the environment. Can you see some examples?

Pipelines and cables can be buried to stop them spoiling the landscape. Roads and railways can be hidden in cuttings or tunnels.

Oil slicks

In 1989 a ship called the *Exxon Valdez* ran aground in Alaska. The ship was an oil tanker and the oil spilled into the sea making an oil slick. Much of the oil reached the coast and killed many animals.

The owners of the tanker paid for the oil to be cleaned up. Cleaning up oil is difficult. It can be burned, cleaned with chemicals and skimmed from the water. A rough sea helps break up oil slicks too.

A sea-bird covered in oil from the Exxon Valdez.

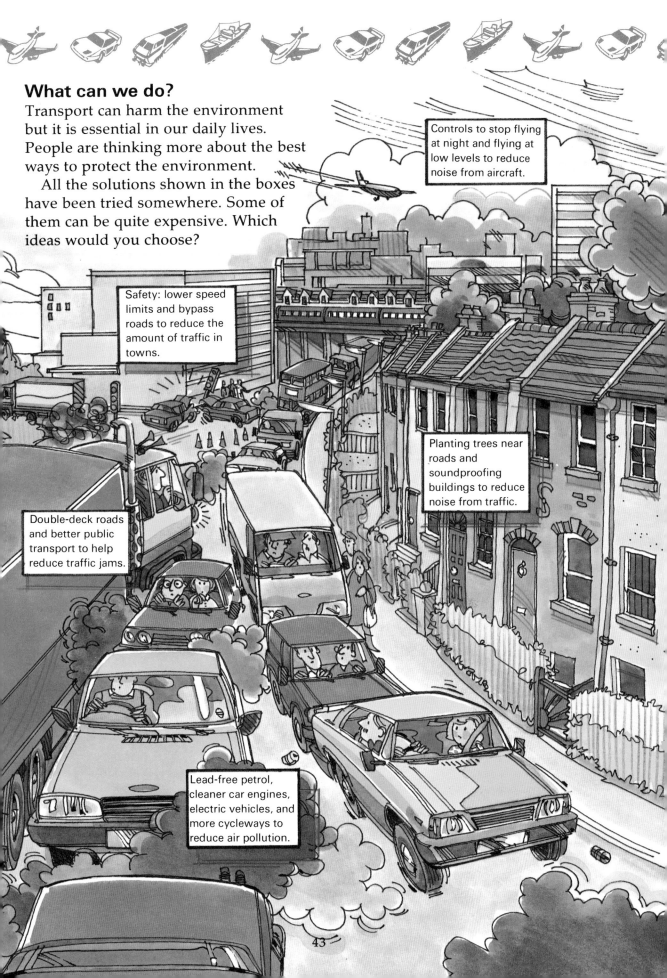

What can we do?

Transport can harm the environment but it is essential in our daily lives. People are thinking more about the best ways to protect the environment.

All the solutions shown in the boxes have been tried somewhere. Some of them can be quite expensive. Which ideas would you choose?

Controls to stop flying at night and flying at low levels to reduce noise from aircraft.

Safety: lower speed limits and bypass roads to reduce the amount of traffic in towns.

Planting trees near roads and soundproofing buildings to reduce noise from traffic.

Double-deck roads and better public transport to help reduce traffic jams.

Lead-free petrol, cleaner car engines, electric vehicles, and more cycleways to reduce air pollution.

Technology of the future

Transport is essential. Without it our lives would be very different. Energy is needed for vehicles to move and most of this energy comes from oil. One day the oil will run out. Engineers are looking for ways of conserving oil – making it go further. Here are some of the ideas, many of which have been tried.

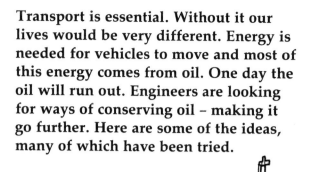

Free energy

Ships are again using the energy of the wind. Modern sailing ships have sails shaped like aerofoils – like the wings of a plane. Air flowing across the sails thrusts the ship forward. Winds, however, are not always reliable. These ships still need an engine. To make the best use of the wind the sails can be moved by computer.

A bit of a drag

Boats waste energy because of the friction or 'drag' of the water. If a boat can be lifted out of the water there is less drag.

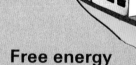

The **hovercraft** floats on a cushion of air.

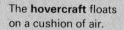

The **catamaran** has two hulls which make it very stable.

The **hydrofoil** skims along the surface on feet called foils.

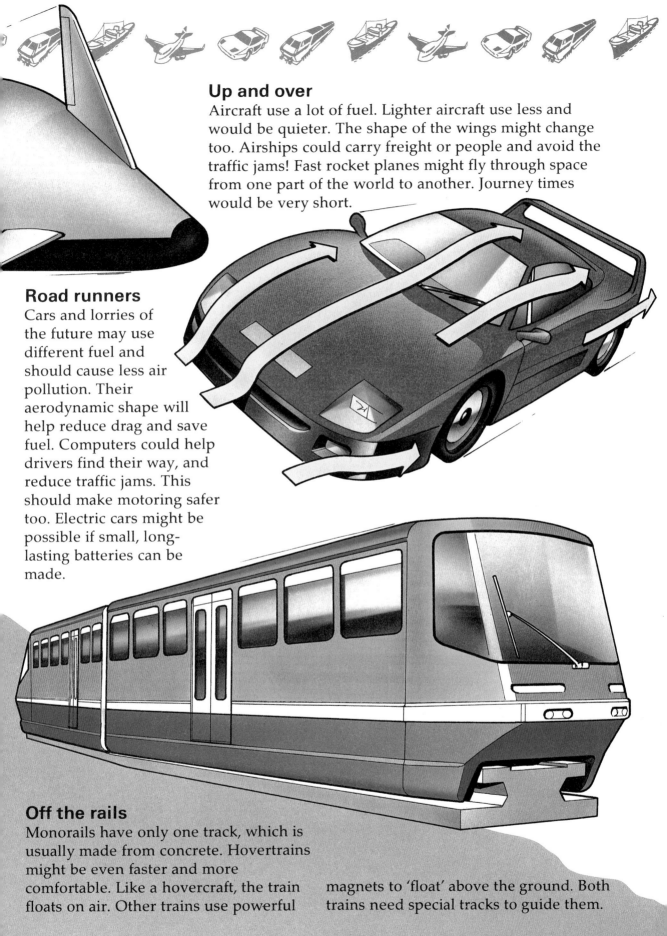

Up and over

Aircraft use a lot of fuel. Lighter aircraft use less and would be quieter. The shape of the wings might change too. Airships could carry freight or people and avoid the traffic jams! Fast rocket planes might fly through space from one part of the world to another. Journey times would be very short.

Road runners

Cars and lorries of the future may use different fuel and should cause less air pollution. Their aerodynamic shape will help reduce drag and save fuel. Computers could help drivers find their way, and reduce traffic jams. This should make motoring safer too. Electric cars might be possible if small, long-lasting batteries can be made.

Off the rails

Monorails have only one track, which is usually made from concrete. Hovertrains might be even faster and more comfortable. Like a hovercraft, the train floats on air. Other trains use powerful magnets to 'float' above the ground. Both trains need special tracks to guide them.

Transport detectives

Explorers travelled to many places to find out what the world was like. Now people want to know more about space and the ocean depths. Knowing how people used to live is also important. It helps us to understand more about our lives today.

Finding out about the past is like being a detective. There are puzzles to be solved and clues to help. These clues are called evidence. Some evidence is easy to spot. Other evidence is more difficult to find – you need to know where to look. Horses were an important form of transport in the past, but how do we know this?

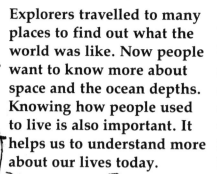

Street furniture
There are still many reminders in our streets of the days of horse transport.

A Stone or granite bollards protected buildings and gateways from horse-drawn vehicles.

B Horses were tied up to tethering rings outside buildings.

C Water troughs and fountains made from cast iron or stone were used for watering horses and other animals.

D Mounting blocks made from stone were used to help riders mount their horses or for passengers to board a carriage.

Buildings
Buildings give you clues that horse transport was once important. A mews is a street lined by stables.

Reading the signs
Road names and inn signs sometimes reveal links with horses too.

Canals

There are many clues along canals which indicate that horses were once used to pull boats.

(A) How do you think the grooves on this bridge were caused?

(B) Why do canals have a path running alongside them?

(C) Why do you think this bridge is split?

(Answers below)

Papers and paintings

Books, magazines, paintings and newspapers can be good sources of information about transport in the past. Old advertisements and posters for vehicles and horse equipment are interesting too.

People

Some older people can remember the days when horse-drawn transport was used in towns and in the countryside. Talking to them about their memories is a good way to find out about the past.

Answers
Horses walked alongside the towpath pulling barges (B). The ropes used to attach the horses to the barges rubbed on walls and bridges, making grooves (A). Bridges were split so that a horse could cross from one side of the canal to the other without having the rope unfastened (C).

Your investigation

You might like to do a bit of transport detective work yourself. The clues on these pages will give you some ideas on where to start. Don't wander around on your own. Ask an adult whom you know well to go with you. Visit transport museums and heritage sites. Ask the librarian at your local library to help you find books and documents. You could record your findings in a file. Remember also that there are many different forms of transport around the world. Keep your eyes open on your travels!

Index

*Numbers in **bold** indicate illustrations.*

Published by BBC Educational Publishing, a division of BBC Enterprises Limited, Woodlands, 80 Wood Lane, London W12 0TT

First published 1992
© Ian Wolseley/BBC Enterprises Ltd 1992
The moral rights of the author have been asserted.
Paperback ISBN: 0 563 347 93 7
Hardback ISBN: 0 563 347 94 5
Typeset by Ace Filmsetting Ltd, Frome, Somerset
Colour reproduction by Daylight Colour, Singapore
Cover origination in England by Dot Gradations
Printed and bound by BPCC Hazell Books, Paulton

Photo credits
Page 3 London Transport Museum; 12 British Waterways Archives; 14 Royal Holloway & Bedford New College Bridgeman Art Library; 17 Popperfoto; 19 Adrian Meredith Photography; 23 Panos Pictures (top), Luke Finn (middle left), South Yorkshire Transport Ltd (middle right), Greyhound Lines Inc (bottom left), London Transport Museum (bottom right); 24 Üstra; 26 London Transport Museum (left); BC Transit (right); 32 Australian National Railways; 36 Hulton Picture Company; 39 Aerofilms Ltd (centre); London Transport Museum (bottom); 41 Zefa Picture Library; 42 Sipa Press.

Front cover *Main picture* The Image Bank/Sheryl S. Honee; *inset top left* Üstra; *top right* Raleigh Industries Ltd; *bottom left* P & O Cruises Ltd; *bottom right* Volvo Trucks (GB) Ltd.